Ralph Gibson

L'HISTOIRE DE FRANCE

INTRODUCTION BY MARGUERITE DURAS

THE PROFESSIONAL PHOTOGRAPHY DIVISION OF EASTMAN KODAK COMPANY
APERTURE

L'Histoire de France accompanies an exhibition by the same
name, which opens at Leo Castelli Gallery in New York in May
1991 and will be travelling internationally.

This Publication is underwritten by the Professional
Photography Division of Eastman Kodak Company through its
continuing support of photography in Journalism.

Library of Congress Catalog Number: 90-08495
Hardcover ISBN: 0-89381-471-7

Aperture, Inc. publishes a periodical, books, and portfolios
of fine photography to communicate with serious
photographers and creative people everywhere. A complete
catalog is available upon request. Address: 20 East 23rd
Street, New York, New York 10010.

Red is the shadow of black

Dear Ralph Gibson:

I've looked many times, again and again, at your book: FRANCE. It's magnificent, Ralph, at the same time violent and of a subtlety that is essential. The magical thing here is that, the more one looks at your work on France, the more one sees it.

One can speak here about a photographic writing: untranslatable, irreversible, with a savage intelligence, profoundly mysterious.

One says to oneself: what one sees there is perhaps what children see, what is called by that staggering word: the real. You have taken the real, from yourself, R.G., and you have taken off with it, onto French soil, the Parisian pavement, the nakedness of the earth between the rows of vines; what is never expressed except, rarely, in poetry.

You have taken no notice of monumental France; I am quite happy about that, really quite happy about that. Who now looks at photos of the Eiffel Tower—as everyone knows, it's only foreigners who still look at it, this Tower, in order to rediscover the most photographed thing in the world. And that's why they look at it—the Tower—they're conducting a kind of verification. Myself, I've always dreamt of seeing a bolt from the Eiffel Tower fallen to the ground, and made into the object of a photograph. But the smoked fish on the background of a BLUE SHIRT, I could not have imagined it.

It's a fish, a herring, which has been caught in a fisherman's net, and then smoked. It happened in the Côtes-du-Nord—that is where the drama took place. It's called *bouffi*, which means the puffed-up one. It is placed in a wooden container to dry along with its other colleagues. It is eaten grilled with unpeeled potatoes, very hot, and fresh butter.

Ralph Gibson's *bouffi* has an extraordinarily alive eye; it looks at the great blue, fixed on the light blue shirt. The joy of its gaze: it believes it has rediscovered the sea of its childhood, the French coastline. Myself, it makes me cry, this herring.

And then there is this woman who is everywhere in R.G.'s books: her face is between twenty and ten thousand years old. She is naked. She looks at no one. She faces the desert. She is beyond R.G., toward the South. Sometimes her eyes are closed. Sometimes almost closed. Between the two eyelids, the sun flows like water. This woman is alone with Bocuse and Lumière, in the book of photographs, in France.

The word "France" on a book of photographs in which one recognizes nothing is something which I recognize completely: therefore everything. France becomes something which provokes a great deal of thought.

For example, myself, what makes me think—I must say in amazement—is the enormous bottle of red wine from BORDEAUX, truncated, as solitary as all wine bottles in cellars or in trains, in ocean liners, in planes. But Ralph's bottle alone will be seen the world over. It's the first time in one's life that one sees the glass of wine not yet come to pass, and it's the first time no doubt that one will remember the fragrance of this miracle wine. Our happiness, good and evil mixed together.

There are no bars in R.G.'s book, no cafés, no place where wine is drunk; there is only this very solitary bottle which shines forth in this unknown place, solitary like a queen, abstract like happiness, indecipherable.

There are also objects caught on the fly. I am thinking of that photo of yours (where did I see it?) which still moves me when I think about it. There. It's a step on an exterior staircase which seems as if it should lead to a park, very lightly warped by time, maybe centuries; and on which, the day and hour of your passage, there was, on this immaculate step, a lost object, tiny and of a common, practical nature: I am referring to the kind of button which fastens men's shirts and women's blouses. A button which is there for a very short time, a couple of hours, and you, you saw this pearly detail. You photographed it very small in the white tide of the step. You photographed the eternity of this detail before the dump trucks took it far away from everything. It was on this step for only a few hours and you signed its eternity as a "button lost by an unknown person in a city of twelve million inhabitants."

What a joy, Ralph, to write about your photographs; you should make me a book and I would write about the unknown in the world and in you, about the mysterious modesty of objects, about the enticement of the red of wine, the perfect insignificance of this lost object and all those fabrics, brocade and cotton mingled together, and the beauty of the buttocks of that woman who is looking toward the South, who can be found between Bocuse and Lumière—everything mingled together, everything, in the great democracy of galaxies.

You have captured the beauty which happens to be France since you call it that, and this without any reverence, any prejudice. You have photographed what cannot be photographed: the spirit of wine, and ourselves in front of the spectacle of life. You are a savage Ralph Gibson and you are my friend.

Marguerite Duras
(PARIS, OCTOBER–NOVEMBER 1990.)

TRANSLATED BY JEAN-CHRISTOPHE CASTELLI

LE FLEUVE

LE PROBLÈME

LES MOTS

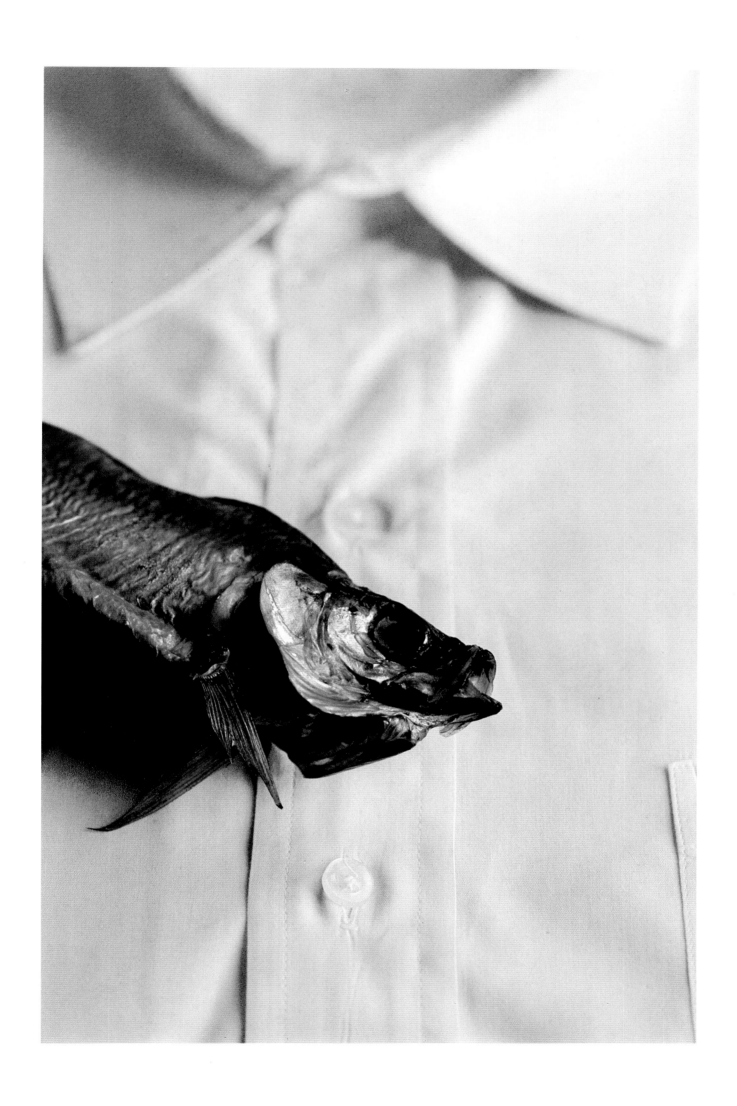

LA FORÊT

LE TIMBRE

LE POISSON

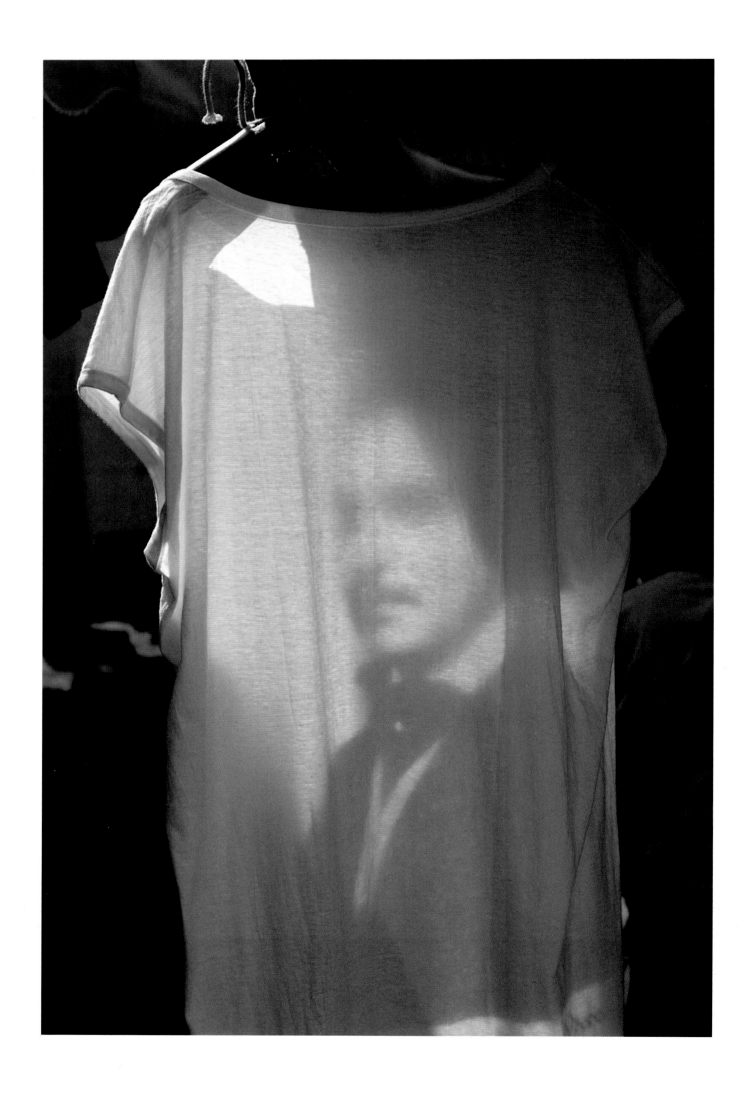

LE JARDIN

LA BOÎTE

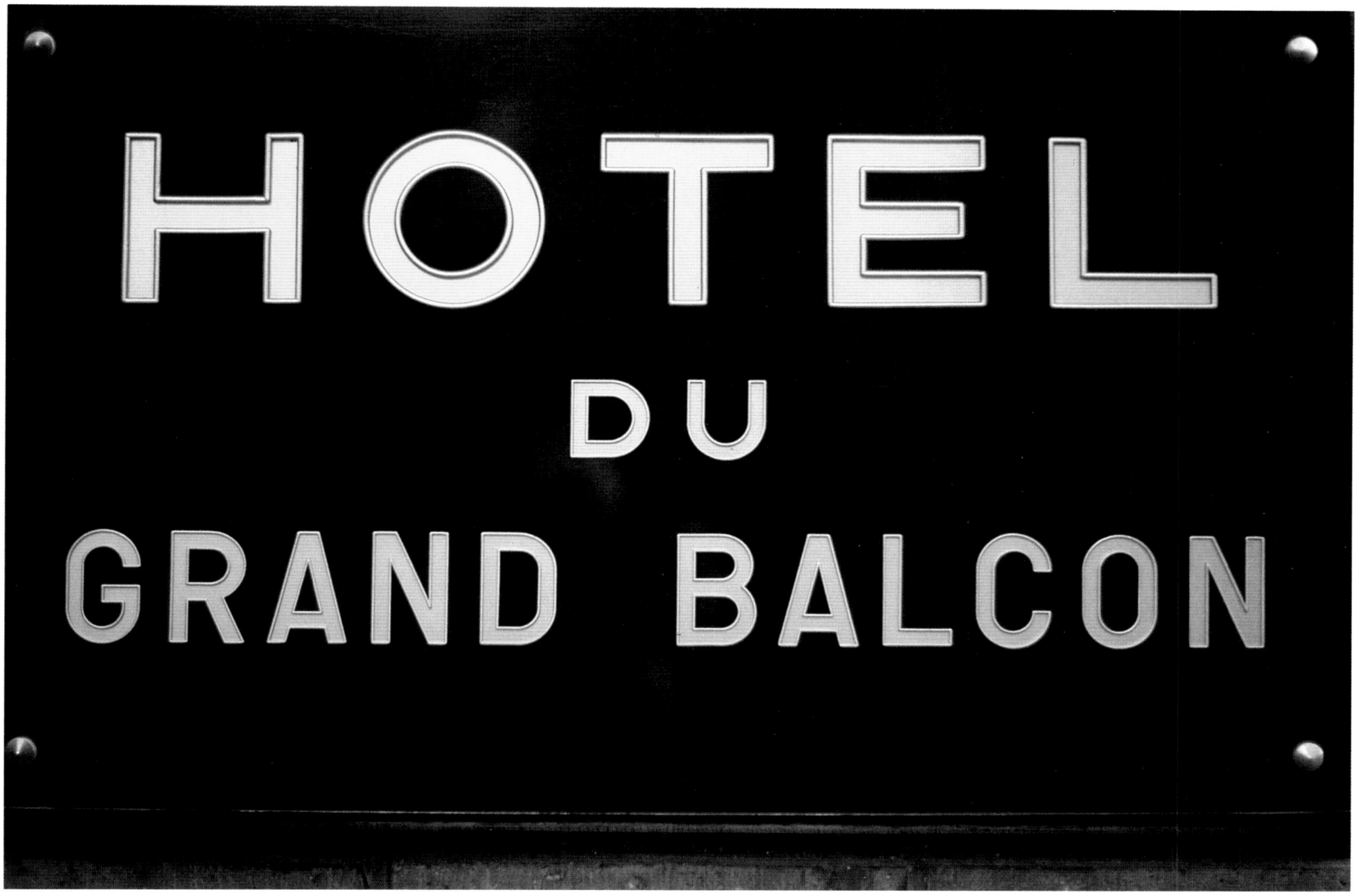
HOTEL
DU
GRAND BALCON

LA CÔTE

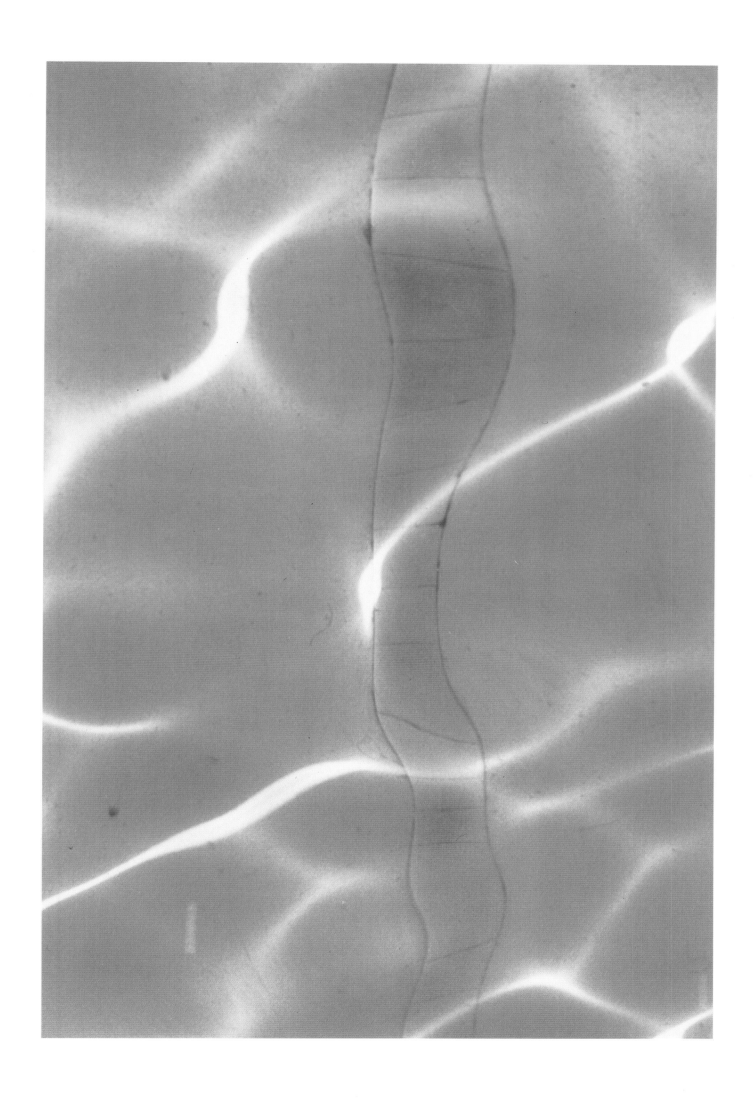

LE PHOTOGRAPHE

Europe is his favorite hunting ground. And France, along, perhaps, with Italy, the country which he apprehends the best. Here, then, in color, with its ambitious and very conventional title, is this *History of France* offered up by a Californian who is a great raconteur, earthy, rakish, of immoderate appetites, larger than life. What a challenge for this photographer obsessed with the minimalists, with the *nouveau roman*, with the aesthetic of effacement! He brings us back a France that has been purified, without paraphrase, without chatter, still and serene — a France forgotten from having been over-frequented. He fixes colors, blurs, forms, signs, allusions. He steals those marks which the French no longer see: a Legion of Honor on the lapel of a suit, the starched *toque* of a great chef, a yellow line next to a gutter, the curve of a bistro table. Caillebotte spoke of the gray of the Parisian pavement; Gibson delivers us its essence. And what if that, precisely, were the gaze of the photographer? The eye of the stranger, of the anthropologist, crossed with a tight-rope philosopher. And what if that, precisely, were what we call the visual signature of Ralph Gibson?

Annie Cohen-Solal
FRENCH CULTURAL COUNSELLOR
FOR THE UNITED STATES

TRANSLATED BY JEAN-CHRISTOPHE CASTELLI

"One does not choose one's subject matter; one submits to it . . ." FLAUBERT

I wish to offer special gratitude to Ray de Moulin and the staff of the Professional Photography division at the Eastman Kodak Company. A very warm "merci" to my long-time friend Marguerite Duras for her splendid introduction. I also thank Annie Cohen-Solal, French Cultural Counsellor for the United States, for her perceptive afterword. Both texts were faithfully translated from the French by Jean-Christophe Castelli. Travels in France were assisted by my colleague Yves Guillot. Thanks are offered to Michel Troche of the Ministry of Culture and Communication of France and to Miles Barth who encouraged the project in many ways. Beth Schiffer made the numerous C-type prints for the book layout and Nino Mondhe made the superb Dye Transfer prints for the portfolio and exhibition. Arne Lewis designed the typography and layout and once again it has been a pleasure working together. This is also very true of all those at Aperture who have endeavored to make the book a reality. Appreciation goes to the Hotel Saint-Simon, Paris, the Hotel Grand Palais, Biarritz, the Maison Pierre Loti, Rochefort and the Domaine de la Faye, Riberac.

An artist in a foreign land is never excused.

Dedicated to Cat, my unknown friend . . .